April 13, 1992

Market-Share Quotas

1. Introduction

Successive rounds of GATT negotiations have reduced the importance of tariffs as a policy instrument for protecting domestic industry. Nontariff barriers have emerged in their place, and prominent among them are quantitative restrictions such as quotas, voluntary restraint agreements, and orderly marketing arrangements.[1] More recently, policymakers have experimented with a new type of protective policy which can be referred to as a "market-share quota". As opposed to a pure restriction on the quantity of imports, this restraint limits imports to a specified percentage of the market. In the United States, this policy came into prominence as a remedy for the section 201 trade complaint brought by the United Steelworkers of America and Bethlehem Steel Corporation. The settlement of this complaint, achieved through a series of bilateral negotiations with major steel-producing nations, restricted imports of carbon and alloy steel to 18.5 percent of U.S. apparent consumption.[2]

After the United States imposed market-share quotas on steel imports in 1984, a curious phenomenon occurred. Evidence indicates that the quotas

---

[1] See Baldwin (1987), Bhagwati (1988), and Abreu (1989).

[2] In 1984, export restraint agreements for steel products were negotiated bilaterally with Japan, South Korea, Spain, Brazil, South Africa, Mexico, Australia, and Finland. At the time of the section 201 case, the European Community had already agreed to voluntary restraints. The agreements with South Africa, Mexico, Australia, and Finland did not directly result from the section 201 case, but "unfair" trade complaints were under active consideration against those countries. The voluntary restraints were renegotiated in 1989; these agreements permitted a one-percent annual increase in the share of imports in U.S. steel consumption. For details, see U.S. International Trade Commission (1991a) and Tarr and Morkre (1984).

1

were not often filled to their limits. For instance, from October 1989 through December 1990, foreign firms only filled 74 percent of their quotas.[3] Of course, changes in the relative cost positions of domestic and foreign producers may have altered the distribution of steel output in a manner that rendered the quota nonbinding. Factors such as the depreciation of the dollar and the modernization of domestic steel-producing plant and equipment may have improved the competitive stance of U.S. producers after the quotas were implemented.[4] Notwithstanding these explanations, an interesting question arises for both theoretical and empirical investigation: "Would the imposition of a market-share quota alter the behavior of domestic and foreign firms in a manner that causes these quotas to remain unfilled?"

This question is important because policymakers often presume that a quota has been ineffective if it is found to be subsequently nonbinding. Although economists may believe otherwise, they often encounter difficulties in distinguishing whether a change in firm behavior or a change in cost and demand conditions has rendered the quota nonbinding. Hence, identifying any likely changes in firm behavior, and their associated welfare effects, is essential to evaluating the success of any quantitative restriction.

This paper attempts to unravel the mystery of the "unfilled" market-share quotas from a theoretical perspective. It examines how the imposition of a market-share quota affects the strategic behavior of domestic and

---

[3] See U.S. International Trade Commission (1991b).

[4] In exchange for import restraints, U.S. steel producers were directed to commit "all of their net cash flow from steel operations to reinvestment and modernization" ("sense of the Congress" resolution included in the Trade and Tariff Act of 1984). It is unclear whether this resolution has affected the investment behavior of U.S. steel producers.

2

foreign firms. In markets with imperfect competition, this policy changes strategic behavior considerably. A market-share quota limits imports to a given percentage of the market -- thus, this policy merely sets a maximum level for the _ratio_ of import sales to domestic sales. This _ratio constraint_ must be translated to a _constraint on the absolute quantity_ of import sales, _but that can only occur after domestic firms have committed to a given quantity of sales_. To the extent that a domestic firm commits to a given quantity of sales through the chosen level of a strategic variable such as output or capacity, _it can use that choice to determine the severity of the market-share quota as a quantitative restriction_.

To illustrate how a market-share quota affects strategic behavior, a Cournot duopoly is examined with one domestic firm and one foreign firm. When the market-share constraint is actually binding, the foreign firm desires to sell more of its output in the home market. Any increase in the domestic firm's sales then raises the permitted level of imports, and is therefore matched by a corresponding increase in the foreign firm's sales. This reaction dampens the incentive for the domestic firm to commit to higher sales by increasing its output. However, once the domestic firm commits to a sufficiently high sales level, the foreign firm can sell all that it desires to the home market without exceeding the market-share limit. Since the foreign firm's sales are no longer constrained by the quota, the domestic firm now expects that an increase in its sales will not induce any change in foreign sales. This result implies that the domestic firm's conjecture about rival behavior changes once its sales reach a sufficiently high level.

Technically, this change in conjectures implies that the domestic

3

firm's profit function is no longer globally concave. The domestic firm thus considers two possible strategies in choosing its output: (1) commit to a low sales level and use the quota to effectively constrain imports, or (2) commit to a high sales level and foresake using the quota as an effective import constraint. The domestic firm prefers one of these strategies, or is indifferent between these two strategies, depending on the output commitment made by the foreign firm. Our results show that the domestic firm uses the quota as an effective constraint at high levels of foreign output, and then foresakes the quota constraint at low levels of foreign output. Due to this discrete change in the strategy used by the domestic firm, no pure-strategy equilibrium exists when the quota is set at or below the free-trade foreign market share.[5]

The only possible equilibrium involves a mixed strategy by the domestic firm -- the nature of this equilibrium explains why a market-share quota is not always filled. The foreign firm's optimal response to the mixed domestic strategy implies that the quota is not filled when the domestic firm follows its "high output" (i.e., "unconstrained") strategy. In contrast, the quota does constrain the foreign firm's sales to the home market when the domestic firm follows its "low output" (i.e., "constrained") strategy.

Relative to a tariff that restricts the foreign firm's market share

---

[5] The lack of a pure-strategy equilibrium under a market-share quota contradicts the common belief that quotas and tariffs produce identical effects in simple Cournot models. In price-setting models, Krishna (1989) and Dean and Gangopadhyay (1991) have shown that the imposition of a quota, or the threat of imposition, eliminates a pure-strategy equilibrium. Quantity-setting models are presumed to be less prone to this problem, although Reitzes (1991) shows that the imposition of a quota may preclude a pure-strategy equilibrium in a multistage game where firms choose both R&D and output.

to an equivalent level, domestic profits are higher and domestic consumer surplus is lower under the market-share quota. Social welfare is lower when the domestic firm uses its "constrained" strategy, but it may be higher when the domestic firm uses its "unconstrained" strategy.

These results often continue to hold when the foreign firm has the ability to shift output across markets subsequent to the domestic firm's output commitment. However, under these conditions, it is instead possible that a pure-strategy equilibrium occurs where the domestic and foreign firms split monopoly profits according to the market shares given by the quota. Social welfare in unambiguously lower in this equilibrium than in that obtained under an equally restrictive tariff.

This paper is organized as follows. Section 2 describes the model. Section 3 analyzes the effect of a market-share quota on the reaction functions of the domestic and foreign firms. Section 4 solves for an equilibrium and presents welfare results. Section 5 considers the effect on these results when the foreign firm can transfer output across markets. Section 6 offers concluding remarks.

2.   The Model

Consider a market served by one domestic firm and one foreign firm. These firms compete in a single-period Cournot duopoly game, where both firms set output levels simultaneously.[6] We assume that the goods are perfect substitutes; however, similar reasoning would apply to imperfect substitutes. Profits for each firm are described as follows (where capital

---

[6] Under appropriate assumptions, the results of our model are not substantively changed if firms set capacity levels instead of output levels.

letters denote the foreign firm):

$$\pi(x,X) = p(x+X)x - c(x) \tag{1}$$

$$\Pi(x,X) = p(x+X)X - C(X), \tag{2}$$

where p is the inverse demand function, c(C) is the domestic(foreign) cost function, and x(X) is domestic(foreign) output. The corresponding first-order conditions are:

$$\pi_x = p + p'x - c_x = 0 \tag{3}$$

$$\Pi_X = p + p'X - C_X = 0, \tag{4}$$

where ' denotes the derivative of the inverse demand function.

We presume that conditions are satisfied so that a unique, stable equilibrium exists. Specifically, it is assumed that:

$$\pi_{xx} < \pi_{xX} < 0; \quad \Pi_{XX} < \Pi_{Xx} < 0. \tag{i}$$

Condition (i) implies that the reaction functions are decreasing with respect to rival output.[7]

Let $x^N(X)$ and $X^N(x)$ represent the Cournot reaction functions for the domestic and foreign firms, respectively. We denote the free-trade Cournot-Nash equilibrium as $(x_f, X_f) = (x^N(X_f), X^N(x_f))$. For future reference, k_f denotes the free-trade market share of the foreign firm.

---

[7] If marginal revenue is decreasing with respect to rival output, then $\pi_{xX}, \Pi_{Xx} < 0$. It follows that $\pi_{xx} < \pi_{xX} < 0$ and $\Pi_{XX} < \Pi_{Xx} < 0$ unless marginal costs are rapidly decreasing. Based on these conditions, the equilibrium must be unique and stable (see Hahn 1962 and Rosen 1965).

3.   The Effect of a Market-Share Quota on Reaction Functions

Prior to the output stage, let the policymaker commit to a market-share quota k, where $0 < k < 1$. If $X^{\sim}$ represents the quantity of foreign sales to the home market, then the quota requires that $X^{\sim}/(x+X^{\sim}) \leq k$, or in other words, $X^{\sim} \leq (k/(1-k))x$. Hence, under a market-share quota, the quantitative limit on foreign sales is increasing with respect to domestic output. Both firms are aware of this relationship in making their output choices. It is still assumed that output choices are made simultaneously, or alternatively, that both firms make their output choices before observing rival behavior.[8]

_____

[8] In contrast, Mai and Hwang (1989) assume that the imposition of a market-share quota (i.e., a ratio quota) necessarily changes firm interaction from simultaneous decisions to Stackelberg leadership by the domestic firm. Accordingly, the domestic firm's output choice maximizes its profits subject to the constraint that its market share equals 1-k. Thus, the domestic firm's best strategy is to force total market sales to the monopoly level, and claim its designated share of monopoly profits.

While this outcome is certainly possible, Mai and Hwang do not explain why Stackelberg behavior would arise endogenously. Moreover, their results rely on the assumption that the market-share quota is binding in equilibrium. This outcome arises only if domestic profits are higher when the domestic firm acts as a "constrained" Stackelberg leader (i.e., one that commits to a "low" output level and uses the quota to effectively constrain imports) than as an "unconstrained" Stackelberg leader (i.e., one that commits to a "high" output level which ultimately renders the quota nonbinding). When the domestic firm acts as an "unconstrained" leader, the traditional Stackelberg equilibrium arises. Since foreign profits may decline significantly in this equilibrium when compared to an equilibrium with simultaneous output choices, the foreign firm is not likely to consent to being a follower. Hence, it is reasonable to suppose that firms still choose outputs simultaneously after the imposition of a market-share quota.

Furthermore, neither firm may observe the other's output choice until that output is brought to market. Under these circumstances, the foreign firm necessarily makes its output choice without knowing the domestic output level and the associated quantitative restriction on its sales. In a one-shot game, this decision process would produce an equilibrium that is identical to that of simultaneous decisions.

3.1 The Foreign Firm's Reaction Function

Consider the impact of the quota on the foreign firm's reaction function. While the domestic firm sells its entire output, the quota may potentially constrain foreign sales to the home market below the foreign output level for that market.[9] For a given domestic output choice, the limit on foreign sales is $X^Q(x,k) = (k/(1-k))x$. When $X \leq X^Q(x,k)$, foreign sales equal foreign output (i.e., $X^\sim = X$). When $X > X^Q(x,k)$, foreign sales are instead constrained at the quota limit (i.e., $X^\sim = X^Q(x,k)$).

The foreign firm's revenue is determined by its <u>sales</u> $X^\sim$, but its costs are determined by its <u>output</u> X. Based on the prior discussion, we can now describe foreign profits under the market-share quota:

$$\Pi^Q(x,X,k) = p(x+X^\sim)X^\sim - C(X) \qquad (5)$$

$$\text{where } X^\sim = X \qquad \text{for } X \leq X^Q(x,k)$$

$$= X^Q(x,k) \qquad \text{for } X > X^Q(x,k).$$

---

[9] In this section and the next section, the foreign firm commits to an output level specifically intended for the home market. Either the home market is the only source of demand, or conditions exist that make it prohibitively costly to transfer output across markets once the magnitude of the quantitative restriction becomes known. These conditions may include unique design requirements for individual markets, customer obligations (i.e., explicit and implicit guarantees to customers or distributors through contracts, orders, etc.), or substantial transportation costs from alternative sources of supply. Even if none of these circumstances is present, the above assumption still applies when the foreign firm must commit quantities to each market prior to observing the output level chosen by the domestic firm.

Later, the analysis considers a situation where the foreign firm sells to more than one market and output is perfectly fungible across markets. In this situation, the foreign firm commits to a total output level, and then decides at a latter stage how to optimally allocate that output across markets. Using this framework, it will be shown that the equilibrium results are often qualitatively similar to those derived below.

From the above, $\Pi^Q(x,X,k)$ is continuous with respect to each of its arguments. Differentiating with respect to X, we obtain:

$$\Pi^Q_X(x,X,k) = p + p'X - C_X \qquad \text{for } X < X^Q(x,k) \qquad (6a)$$

$$= - C_X \qquad \text{for } X > X^Q(x,k). \qquad (6b)$$

The expression in (6a) represents marginal profits under a <u>nonbinding</u> quota constraint, and is thus identical to equation (4). Accordingly, the first-order condition from (6a) is solved by the original <u>unconstrained</u> reply, $X^N(x)$. The expression in (6b) is always negative because any foreign output in excess of the quota limit cannot be sold. Based on these results, $X^N(x)$ is an optimal reply whenever it is less than or equal to $X^Q(x,k)$. Whenever $X^N(x)$ is greater than $X^Q(x,k)$, the foreign firm's optimal reply is to set output at the quota limit, $X^Q(x,k)$. We summarize below, where $X^R(x,k)$ denotes the foreign reaction function under the quota:

$$X^R(x,k) = X^N(x) \qquad \text{for } X^N(x) \leq X^Q(x,k)$$

$$= X^Q(x,k) \qquad \text{for } X^N(x) > X^Q(x,k). \qquad (7)$$

The reaction function, $X^R(x,k)$, changes its behavior at the value of x that satisfies $X^N(x) = X^Q(x,k)$. Let $x*(k)$ represent this value, i.e., $x*(k)$ is the domestic output level where the foreign firm's best <u>unconstrained</u> reply equals the quota limit. Since $X^N(x)$ is decreasing in x, while $X^Q(x,k)$ is increasing in x, it holds that $X^N(x) \gtreqless X^Q(x,k)$ if $x \lesseqgtr x*(k)$. Substituting this result into equation (7), we now define the foreign reaction function:

9

Lemma 1: The optimal foreign reply under the quota is:

$$X^R(x,k) = X^Q(x,k) \qquad \text{for } x < x*(k)$$

$$= X^N(x) \qquad \text{for } x \geq x*(k). \qquad (8)$$

Figure 1 displays this reaction function, where the quota is set at the free-trade foreign market share k_f. In this case, $x*(k_f) = x_f$.[10] Note that the reaction function slopes upward for $x < x*(k_f)$, and downward for $x > x*(k_f)$.

The result in Lemma 1 is quite intuitive. At low levels of domestic output, the foreign firm sets output at the quota limit because its best unconstrained reply exceeds the quota. At high levels of domestic output, the foreign firm uses its best unconstrained reply without exceeding the quota. This result occurs because, in the absence of a quota, the foreign firm's market share is decreasing with respect to domestic output when the foreign firm uses its best unconstrained reply.

3.2 The Domestic Firm's Reaction Function

Now, consider the domestic reaction function. The domestic firm can manipulate the quota so that the foreign firm cannot sell its entire output intended for the home market. To see this, let $x^Q(X,k) = ((1-k)/k)X$ (i.e., x^Q is the inverse of X^Q, treating k as a constant). When $x < x^Q(X,k)$,

---

[10] If the domestic firm chooses its free-trade output x_f, and the foreign firm chooses its free-trade output $X^N(x_f)$ (i.e., X_f), then the foreign market share equals the free-trade level k_f. Thus, $X^N(x_f) = X^Q(x_f, k_f)$. Since $x*(k)$ satisfies $X^N(x) = X^Q(x,k)$ for any given k, it follows that $x_f = x*(k_f)$.

10

FIGURE 1

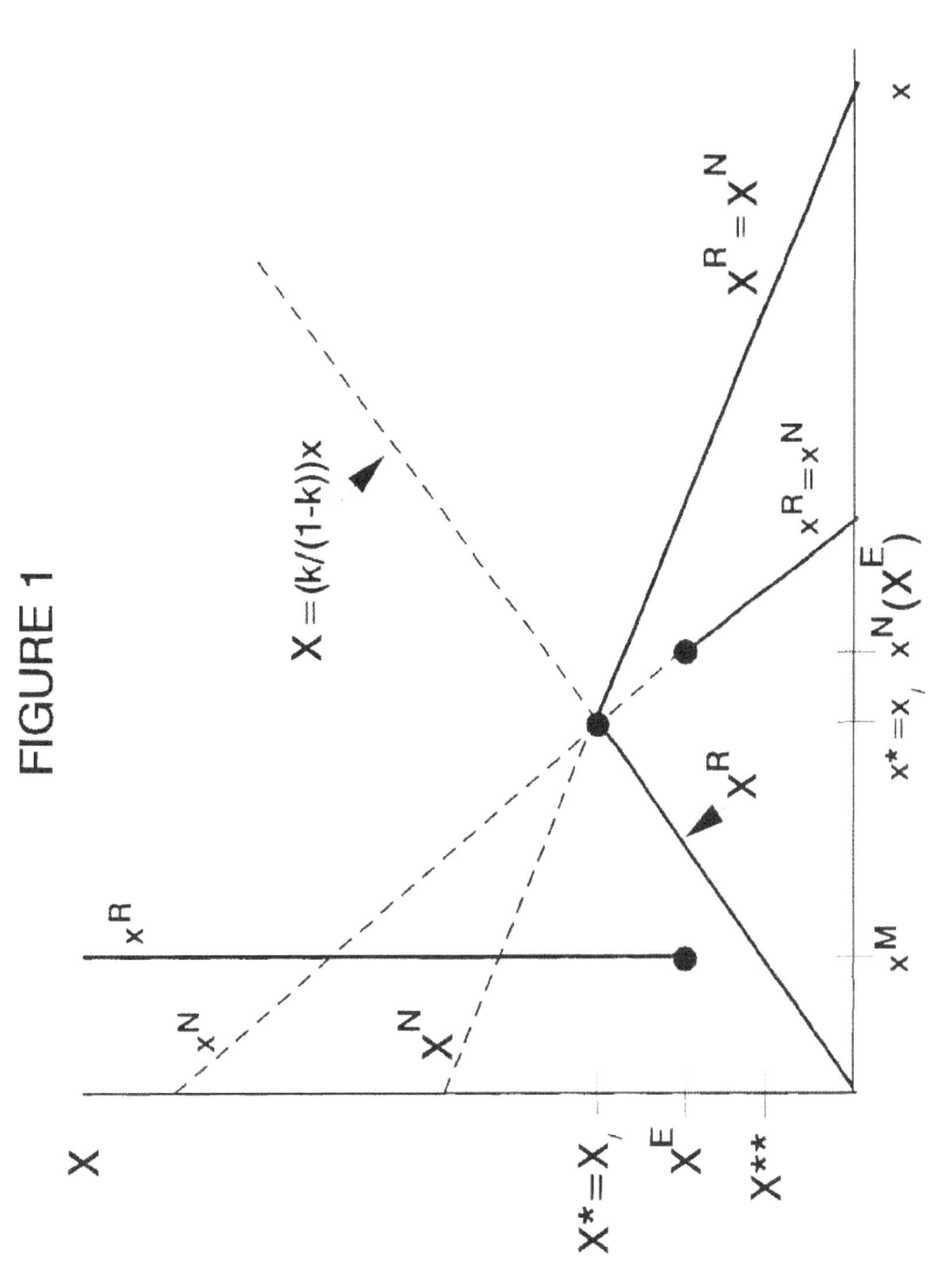

the quota constrains the foreign firm from selling its entire output.[11] Instead, the foreign firm only sells its limit, (i.e., $X^{\sim} = X^Q(x,k)$). When $x \geq x^Q(X,k)$, the foreign firm sells its entire output (i.e., $X^{\sim} = X$). Given that the domestic firm always sells its entire output, the following expression represents domestic profits under the market-share quota:

$$\pi^Q(x,X,k) = p(x+X^{\sim})x - c(x), \qquad (9)$$

where $X^{\sim} = X^Q(x,k)$ for $x < x^Q(X,k)$

            $= X$ for $x \geq x^Q(X,k)$.

From the above, $\pi^Q(x,X,k)$ is continuous with respect to each of its arguments. Recalling that $X^Q(x,k) = (k/(1-k))x$, we differentiate equation (9) with respect to x:

$$\pi^Q_x(x,X,k) = p + p'x(1 + k/(1-k)) - c_x \quad \text{for } x < x^Q(X,k) \qquad (10a)$$

$$= p + p'x - c_x \qquad\qquad\qquad \text{for } x > x^Q(X,k). \qquad (10b)$$

The expression in (10a) represents marginal profits under a <u>binding</u> quota constraint. The expression in (10b) represents marginal profits under a <u>nonbinding</u> quota constraint, and is thus identical to equation (3).

Since $p'x(k/(1-k)) < 0$, it follows from (10a) and (10b) that $\pi^Q_x(x,X,k)$ makes an upward jump at $x^Q(X,k)$. This jump occurs because the domestic firm changes its conjecture concerning the reaction of foreign sales to an increase in its output. When $x < x^Q(X,k)$, the quota limit is less than the foreign output level. Within this range, any expansion in domestic output leads to a corresponding increase in foreign <u>sales</u> because

---

[11] If $x < x^Q(X,k)$, then by definition, $x < ((1-k)/k)X$. Hence, $X > (k/(1-k))x$, or by definition, $X > X^Q(x,k)$. Foreign output thus exceeds the quota limit.

it raises the _quantity_ of foreign sales allowed by the market-share quota. Thus, the foreign firm can sell more of its available output. By contrast, when $x > x^Q(X,k)$, the quota limit exceeds the foreign output level. Within this range, any expansion in domestic output does not affect foreign sales since the foreign firm already sells its entire output. According to this reasoning, the reaction of foreign sales to an expansion in domestic output is positive for $x < x^Q(X,k)$ and zero for $x > x^Q(X,k)$. This behavior causes the marginal value of domestic output to jump upward at $x^Q(X,k)$.

The upward jump in $\pi^Q_x(x,X,k)$ implies that $\pi^Q(x,X,k)$ must be convex in the neighborhood of $x^Q(X,k)$; hence, domestic profits cannot attain a maximum at $x^Q(X,k)$. In other words, _it is never optimal for the domestic firm to set its output so that the foreign firm's output is at the quota limit. Therefore, no pure-strategy equilibrium occurs where the foreign firm sets output at the quota limit, $X^Q(x,k)$._

The imposition of a market-share quota implies that $\pi^Q(x,X,k)$ is not _globally_ concave with respect to x. However, since we can reasonably assume that $\pi^Q_{xx} < 0$ for $x \neq x^Q(x,k)$, it follows that $\pi^Q(x,X,k)$ is "_piecewise_" concave.[12] Thus, only two output choices can potentially maximize domestic profits. One choice, $x^M(k)$, satisfies the first-order condition from (10a). We refer to this choice, which maximizes domestic profits under the constraint that the domestic firm always supplies the market share 1-k, as

---

[12] Our prior assumptions ensure that $\pi^Q_{xx} < 0$ for $x > x^Q(X,k)$. Also, $\pi^Q_{xx} < 0$ for $x < x^Q(X,k)$ if industry marginal revenue is declining and marginal costs are nondecreasing (see next footnote). It follows that $\pi(x,X,k)$ is concave in x for the two "pieces," $x \leq x^Q(X,k)$ and $x \geq x^Q(X,k)$.

12

the best <u>constrained</u> strategy.[13] The other choice, $x^N(X)$, satisfies the first-order condition from (10b). We refer to this choice, which is the same output as that chosen in the absence of a quota, as the best <u>unconstrained</u> strategy.

It is easy to determine which of these two strategies leads to higher profits. Two cases are readily identifiable. First, if the choice of domestic output indicated by the best <u>unconstrained</u> strategy would actually make the quota <u>binding</u>, then the domestic firm instead maximizes profits by using its best <u>constrained</u> strategy. More precisely, at all values of X where $x^N(X) \leq x^Q(X,k)$, it holds that $x^M(k)$ is the optimal domestic reply.[14]

Let $X*(k)$ solve $x^N(X) = x^Q(X,k)$ -- i.e., $X*(k)$ is the foreign output level where if the domestic firm uses its best <u>unconstrained</u> strategy, then foreign output is at the quota limit. Since $x^N(X)$ is decreasing in X while $x^Q(X,k)$ is increasing in X, it follows that $x^N(X) \leq x^Q(X,k)$ for $X \geq X*(k)$. Thus, according to the prior discussion, $x^M(k)$ is the optimal domestic reply for $X \geq X*(k)$. Given this domestic reply, the foreign firm is unable to

---

[13] Using this strategy, total market consumption is close to the level obtained if the domestic firm were a monopolist. To see this, note that the first-order condition from (10a) implies that $p + p'(x+X^\sim) - c_x(x) = 0$ (since $X^\sim = (k/(1-k))x$ in a "constrained" equilibrium). Given that $x+X^\sim$ represents total market sales, a domestic monopolist satisfies the same first-order condition except that $c_x(x+X^\sim)$ replaces $c_x(x)$. This result is sensible because maximizing the profits of a firm with a constant market share is similar to maximizing total industry profits.

[14] Dropping the functional arguments, let $x^N \leq x^Q$. Since x^N satisfies $p + p'x - c_x = 0$, and since $p + p'x - c_x$ is declining in x, this assumption implies $\pi^Q_x(x{\Rightarrow}x^{Q+},X,k) = p + p'x^Q - c_x \leq 0$. Given that $p'x^Q(k/(1-k)) < 0$, it holds from equations (10a,b) that $\pi^Q_x(x{\Rightarrow}x^{Q-},X,k) = p + p'x^Q(1+(k/(1-k))- c_x < 0$.

Since $\pi^Q_x(x{\Rightarrow}x^{Q+},X,k) \leq 0$ and $\pi^Q_{xx} < 0$ for $x{\neq}x^Q$, it holds that $\pi^Q_x < 0$ for $x > x^Q$. Since $\pi^Q_x(x{\Rightarrow}x^{Q-},X,k) < 0$ and $\pi^Q_{xx} < 0$ for $x{\neq}x^Q$, it holds that $\pi^Q_x < 0$ for $x^M < x < x^Q$, and that $\pi^Q_x > 0$ for $x < x^M$. Based on the above results, repeated use of the mean-value theorem shows that x^M maximizes profits. Given that $x^M < x^Q$, foreign sales are constrained by the quota.

sell its entire output. It must instead sell only the quota limit.

Second, if the choice of domestic output indicated by the best constrained strategy would actually make the quota nonbinding, then the domestic firm instead maximizes profits by using its best unconstrained strategy. More precisely, at all values of X where $x^M(k) \geq x^Q(X,k)$, it holds that $x^N(X)$ is the optimal domestic reply.[15]

Let $X**(k)$ solve $x^M(k) = x^Q(X,k)$ -- i.e., $X**(k)$ is the foreign output level where if the domestic firm uses its best constrained strategy, then foreign output is at the quota limit. Given that $x^M(k)$ is independent of X, and that $x^Q(X,k)$ is increasing in X, it follows that $x^M(k) \geq x^Q(X,k)$ for $X \leq X**(k)$. Thus, according to the prior discussion, $x^N(X)$ is the optimal domestic reply for $X \leq X**(k)$. Given this domestic reply, the foreign firm can sell its entire output without exceeding the quota limit.

We have just shown that $x^N(X)$ is an optimal reply for $X \leq X**(k)$, and that $x^M(k)$ is an optimal reply for $X \geq X*(k)$. Define $Z(X,k) = \pi^Q(x^M(k),X,k) - \pi^Q(x^N(X),X,k)$ as the difference in domestic profits from using the best "constrained" and "unconstrained" strategies. It follows that $Z(X,k) < 0$ for $X \leq X**(k)$, and that $Z(X,k) > 0$ for $X \geq X*(k)$.

Now, assume temporarily that $Z(X,k)$ is monotonically increasing in X for $X**(k) < X < X*(k)$. If this assumption holds, then it follows from the above results that a unique value of X satisfies $Z(X,k) = 0$. At this value of X, referred to as $X^E(k)$, domestic profits are the same from using either of the two possible optimal domestic strategies. Furthermore, $Z(X,k) <(>) 0$ for $X <(>) X^E(k)$, which implies that $x^N(X)(x^M(k))$ **is the optimal domestic reply for X** $<(>) X^E(k)$. Thus, the domestic reaction function under the

---

[15] The proof is analagous to that used in the previous footnote.

quota is completely described.

In fact, $Z(X,k)$ is monotonically increasing for $X**(k) < X < X*(k)$. Within this range, the foreign firm is unable to sell its entire output if the domestic output response is $x^M(k)$. Hence, domestic profits under the constrained strategy are unaffected by increases in foreign output. By contrast, the foreign firm is able to sell its entire output if the domestic output response is $x^N(X)$.[16] Hence, domestic profits under the unconstrained strategy decline as foreign output increases. Since $\pi^Q(x^M(k),X,k)$ is independent of X and $\pi^Q(x^N(X),X,k)$ is decreasing in X, it follows that $Z(X,k)$ (i.e., $\pi^Q(x^M(k),X,k) - \pi^Q(x^N(X),X,k)$) is increasing in X for $X**(k) < X < X*(k)$. Based on the above discussion, we now describe the domestic reaction function:

Lemma 2: There exists a unique value of X, known as $X^E(k)$, that satisfies $\pi^Q(x^M(k),X,k) - \pi^Q(x^N(X),X,k)$. Further, $X**(k) < X^E(k) < X*(k)$. The optimal domestic reply under the quota is:

$$\mathbf{x}^R(X,k) - x^N(X) \qquad \text{for } X \leq X^E(k)$$

$$- \mathbf{x}^M(k) \qquad \text{for } X \geq X^E(k). \qquad (11)$$

We display this reaction function in Figure 1 for a quota set at the free-trade foreign market share, $k_/$. In this case, $X*(k_/) - X_/$, which implies that $X^E(k_/) < X_/$.

The above lemma has a straightforward interpretation. At high levels

---

[16] Let X satisfy $X**(k) < X < X*(k)$. Since $x^N(X) > x^Q(X,k)$ for $X < X*(k)$, the foreign firm can sell its entire output if the domestic firm chooses $x^N(X)$. Since $x^M(k) < x^Q(X,k)$ for $X > X**(k)$, the foreign firm cannot sell its entire output if the domestic firm chooses $x^M(k)$.

of foreign output, the domestic firm uses a <u>constrained</u> strategy where it uses the quota to <u>constrain</u> foreign <u>sales</u> below the foreign <u>output</u> level. As foreign <u>output</u> falls, the domestic firm's profits from the constrained strategy are unaffected, but its profits from the unconstrained strategy increase. When foreign output reaches a sufficiently low level, both strategies result in the same level of profits. Any further decline in foreign output then causes the domestic firm to use the <u>unconstrained</u> strategy, which renders the quota <u>nonbinding</u>.

4.   <u>Results</u>

Based on our prior discussion, the following proposition can be established:

<u>Proposition 1:</u> No equilibrium exists in pure strategies whenever the quota is set at or below the free-trade foreign market share.

<u>Proof:</u> (informal)   Let (x_o, X_o) represent a potential pure-strategy equilibrium. From Lemma 1, X_o must satisfy either $X^Q(x_o, k)$ or $X^N(x_o)$. We eliminate both strategies as being consistent with equilibrium.

If $X_o = X^Q(x_o, k)$, then by definition, $x_o = x^Q(X_o, k)$. Since $\pi^Q(x, X_o, k)$ is convex with respect to x in the neighborhood of $x^Q(X_o, k)$, it follows that $x_o = x^Q(X_o, k)$ is not an optimal reply to X_o.

If $X_o = X^N(x_o)$ is a best reply for the foreign firm, then foreign output must be at or below the quota limit (see equation (7)). Since no equilibrium exists when foreign output is at the quota limit, <u>foreign output must be below the quota limit</u>. If the quota limit is <u>not</u> binding when the domestic firm is acting optimally, then the domestic firm must be using its best <u>unconstrained</u> strategy, i.e., $x_o = x^N(X_o)$ (see discussion prior to Lemma 2). Hence, $(x_o, X_o) = (x^N(X_o), X^N(x_o))$ describes the only possible equilibrium. This condition is satisfied only at the free-trade output combination, $(x_f, X_f) = (x^N(X_f), X^N(x_f))$. A contradiction exists because if the quota is set at or below the free-trade market share, then this output combination puts <u>foreign output at or above the quota limit</u>. QED

Using Figure 1, we provide some intuition as to why there is no pure-strategy equilibrium. Consider three regions: (a) $X > (k/(1-k))x$, (b) $X = (k/(1-k))x$, and (c) $X < (k/(1-k))x$. No point in region (a) can represent an equilibrium since foreign output exceeds the quota limit. Thus, the foreign firm would earn higher profits by reducing its output. No point in region (b) can represent an equilibrium because foreign output is at the quota limit. As mentioned previously, the domestic profit function is convex with respect to domestic output when foreign output is at the quota limit. Thus, the domestic firm can increase its profits by changing its output. Finally, no point in region (c) can represent an equilibrium if the quota is set at or below the free-trade foreign market share. Region (c) contains only those points where foreign output is below the quota limit. Since the quota constraint is not binding, both firms are acting optimally only if they use their best unconstrained strategies, $x^N(X)$ and $X^N(x)$. When these strategies are used, the only possible equilibrium can occur at the free-trade output combination. However, when the quota is set at or below the free-trade foreign market share, this output combination puts foreign output at or above the quota. This outcome contradicts the fact that foreign output is below the quota in region (c), and thus eliminates any possible equilibrium in that region.

As implied by Figure 1, the absence of a pure-strategy equilibrium

17

does not preclude the existence of a mixed-strategy equilibrium:[17]

Proposition 2:   A unique mixed-strategy equilibrium exists whenever the quota is set at or below the free-trade foreign market share.   In this equilibrium, the foreign firm sets output at $X^E(k)$ as a pure strategy while the domestic firm mixes output choices between $x^M(k)$ and $x^N(X^E(k))$.   When the domestic firm chooses $x^M(k)$, foreign output is above the quota limit (i.e., the foreign firm cannot sell its entire output).   When the domestic firm chooses $x^N(X^E(k))$, foreign output is below the quota limit.

Proof: Refer to Figure 1.   It has been previously shown that at $(x^M(k),X^E(k))$, the foreign firm is unable to sell its entire output.   Thus, $X^E(k) > X^Q(x^M(k),k)$.   It follows from (6b) that $\Pi^Q_X(x^M(k),X^E(k),k) < 0$.

It has been previously shown that at $(x^N(X^E(k)),X^E(k))$, the foreign firm is able to sell its entire output.   Thus, if the domestic firm uses $x^N(X^E(k))$ as a pure strategy, then the optimal foreign reply is $X^N(x^N(X^E(k)))$, where $X^N(x^N(X^E(k)))$ is the value of X that solves $\Pi^Q_X(x^N(X^E(k)),X,k) = 0$.   Further, $X^N(x^N(X^E(k))) > X^E(k)$ for $k \leq k_f$.[18]   Given that $\Pi^Q_X(x^N(X^E(k)),X,k) = 0$ at $X^N(x^N(X^E(k)))$, that $X^N(x^N(X^E(k))) > X^E(k)$,

---

[17]   The existence of a mixed-strategy equilibrium is not surprising. We have shown that there are two possible domestic strategies, "constrained" ($x^M(k)$) and "unconstrained" ($x^N(X)$).   Thus, the domestic firm's strategy space can be redefined as a $[0,1]$ interval, where $\rho \in [0,1]$ represents the probability of using a "constrained" strategy.   The foreign firm's strategy space remains unchanged.   Both of these strategy spaces are compact and convex, and the reaction correspondences are upper hemicontinuous and convex.   Hence, Kakutani's fixed-point theorem establishes the existence of an equilibrium (ρ,X) combination.   See Glicksberg (1952) and Dasgupta and Maskin (1986) for general propositions relating to the existence of mixed-strategy equilibria.

[18]   Since the free-trade equilibrium, $(x_f,X_f) = (x^N(X_f),X^N(x_f))$, requires that $X^N(x^N(X_f)) = X^N(x_f) = X_f$, and since $dX^N(x^N(X))/dX < 1$ (based on the stability condition contained in equation (i)), it follows that $X^N(x^N(X)) > X$ for $X < X_f$.   Hence, $X^N(x^N(X^E(k))) > X^E(k)$ because $X^E(k) < X_f$ for $k \leq k_f$.   To prove that $X^E(k) < X_f$ for $k \leq k_f$, note that: (1) $X*(k) \leq X_f$ for $k \leq k_f$, and (2) $X^E(k) < X*(k)$ for all k (see Lemma 2).

18

and that $\Pi^Q_{XX} < 0$, it follows that $\Pi^Q_X(x^N(X^E(k)),X^E(k),k) > 0$.[19]

Let $Y(\rho,X,k) = \rho\Pi^Q(x^M(k),X,k) + (1-\rho)\Pi^Q(x^N(X^E(k)),X,k)$, where $\rho(1-\rho)$ is the probability that the domestic firm chooses $x^M(k)(x^N(X^E(k)))$. From our prior assumptions, $Y(\rho,X,k)$ is concave in X.[20] Thus, $Y(\rho,X,k)$ attains a maximum if X satisfies $Y_X(\rho,X,k) = 0$.

Since it has been previously shown that $\Pi^Q_X(x^M(k),X^E(k),k) < 0$ and $\Pi^Q_X(x^N(X^E(k)),X^E(k),k) > 0$, there exists $\rho=\rho*$ such that $Y_X(\rho*,X^E(k),k) = 0$. Thus, if the domestic firm chooses $x^M(k)$ with probability $\rho*$ and $x^N(X^E(k))$ with probability $1-\rho*$, the foreign firm maximizes its profits by choosing $X^E(k)$. Since, from Lemma 2, the domestic firm earns the same maximum level of profits by choosing either $x^M(k)$ or $x^N(X^E(k))$ in reply to $X^E(k)$, a mixed-strategy equilibrium arises. QED

The intuition behind Proposition 2 is as follows. Consider two identical firms with constant marginal costs. Let a quota be imposed at the free-trade foreign market share, i.e., $k = k_f = 1/2$. If the foreign firm continues to select its free-trade output X_f, then the domestic firm's best strategy is to reduce its output to $x^M(k_f)$, which represents one half of the monopoly output level. Since the quota constrains foreign sales to the same level as domestic output, this strategy implies that the domestic firm claims one half of monopoly profits instead of one half of Cournot profits.

If the foreign firm tries to avoid "overproduction" by reducing its own output to $x^M(k_f)$, then the domestic firm earns even greater profits by

---

[19] It is possible that $X^Q(x^N(X^E(k)),k)$, not $X^N(x^N(X^E(k)))$, is the optimal reply to $x^N(X^E(k))$. Nonetheless, this result still holds. Since a reply of $X^Q(x^N(X^E(k)),k)$ puts foreign output at the quota limit, while a reply of $X^E(k)$ puts foreign output below the quota limit, it follows that $X^Q(x^N(X^E(k)),k) > X^E(k)$. Moreover, if $X^Q(x^N(X^E(k)),k)$ is an optimal response to $x^N(X^E(k))$, then $\Pi^Q_X(x^N(X^E(k)),X,k) \geq 0$ as $X \Rightarrow X^Q(x^N(X^E(k)),k)^-$. Since $X^E(k) < X^Q(x^N(X^E(k)),k)$, and since $\Pi^Q_{XX} < 0$ for $X < X^Q(x^N(X^E(k)),k)$, it follows from the prior result that $\Pi^Q_X(x^N(X^E(k)),X^E(k),k) > 0$.

[20] Within the relevant range of foreign output choices, this condition holds unless marginal costs _decrease_ rapidly. Moreover, this condition holds globally whenever marginal costs are _nondecreasing_.

boosting output above the original free-trade level and rendering the quota nonbinding. Thus, the domestic firm will not let the foreign firm produce just enough output to reach the quota limit. This behavior eliminates any possibility for a pure-strategy equilibrium.

An equilibrium can occur only if the foreign firm produces more output than $x^M(k_l)$, but less output than X_l. As the foreign firm raises its output above $x^M(k_l)$, it becomes less profitable for the domestic firm to produce sufficient output to render the quota nonbinding. When foreign output reaches $X^E(k_l)$, the domestic firm is indifferent between using quota protection by choosing $x^M(k_l)$, and foresaking quota protection by choosing $x^N(X^E(k_l))$. If the domestic firm mixes these two strategies with appropriate probabilities, then the foreign firm is content to keep its output at $X^E(k_l)$. A mixed-strategy equilibrium is thus attained.

When the domestic firm chooses $x^M(k_l)$ in equilibrium, it uses the quota to constrain foreign sales below the foreign output level. Thus, foreign output necessarily exceeds the quota.[21] In contrast, when the domestic firm chooses $x^N(X^E(k_l))$ in equilibrium, it foresakes quota protection. Foreign output must therefore be below the quota limit. Thus, the mixed-strategy equilibrium implies that the market-share quota is not always filled.

Summarizing, if the foreign firm does not alter its output choice after the imposition of a market-share quota, then the domestic firm will

---

[21] Alternatively, this situation might be viewed as one where the foreign firm "wastes" output in order to reduce the probability that the domestic firm acts opportunistically. Characterizing this equilibrium in the context of an infinitely-repeated game, it is possible that "excess" foreign output is actually held (at positive cost) as "inventories" for use in future periods. This suggests that the imposition of a market-share quota may induce "strategic" inventory behavior by the foreign firm.

use the quota to constrain foreign sales below the foreign output level. With this in mind, the foreign firm reduces output, but only to the point where the domestic firm is indifferent between using quota protection and abandoning quota protection.

Based on the results from Proposition 2, we compare output, prices, and profits in the cum-quota equilibrium with an equally-restrictive cum-tariff (or free-trade) equilibrium:

Proposition 3: Consider a quota set at or below the free-trade foreign market share, i.e., $k \leq k_f$. Relative to a cum-tariff (or free-trade) equilibrium where the foreign market share equals k, it holds under the quota that:

(1) domestic profits are higher and domestic consumer surplus is lower,

(2) market price is higher,

(3) foreign output is lower and domestic output is lower(higher) when the domestic firm chooses $x^M(k)(x^N(X^E(k))$.[22]

Proof: The comparable cum-tariff equilibrium, (x_T, X_T), uniquely satisfies: (1) $x_T = x^N(X_T)$, and (2) $X_T/(x_T + X_T) = X_T/[x^N(X_T) + X_T] = k$. Since, by definition, $X*(k)$ solves $x^N(X*(k)) = x^Q(X*(k), k)$, it holds that $X*(k)/[x^N(X*(k)) + X*(k)] = k$.[23] Thus, conditions (1) and (2) are fulfilled

_____

[22] Even if the foreign firm keeps all quota rents, foreign profits may still be relatively lower under the quota. For instance, when the quota is set at the free-trade foreign market share, foreign profits are lower under the quota if the domestic firm chooses $x^N(X^E(k_f))$ with sufficiently high probability. This result arises because domestic output has increased from the free-trade equilibrium.

[23] Let $x^N(X*(k)) = x^Q(X*(k), k)$. By definition, $x^Q(X*(k), k) = ((1-k)/k)X*(k)$. It follows that $X*(k)/[x^N(X*(k)) + X*(k)] = X*(k)/[x^Q(X*(k), k) + X*(k)] = k$.

21

only if $(x_T, X_T) = (x^N(X*(k)), X*(k))$. Since $X^E(k) < X*(k)$ by Lemma 2, foreign output is lower under the quota.

Consider the domestic reply, $x^N(X^E(k))$. Given that $X^E(k) < X*(k)$, and that $x^N(X)$ is declining in X, it follows that $x^N(X^E(k)) > x^N(X*(k))$. Since $-1 < dx^N(X)/dX < 0$ by condition (i), it also holds that $x^N(X^E(k)) + X^E(k) < x^N(X*(k)) + X*(k)$. These results show that domestic output is higher, but total output is lower under the quota. Hence, price is higher (i.e., consumer surplus is lower). Domestic profits are higher under the quota because foreign output is relatively lower.

Consider the domestic reply, $x^M(k)$. We have shown that this reply is optimal only if it causes foreign sales to be constrained at the quota limit -- i.e., $x^M(k) < x^Q(X^E(k), k)$. Given that $x^Q(X, k)$ is increasing in X, and that $X^E(k) < X*(k)$, it follows that $x^M(k) < x^Q(X^E(k), k) < x^Q(X*(k), k) = x^N(X*(k))$. Since $x^M(k) < x^N(X*(k))$, domestic output is lower under the quota. Given that the foreign market share equals k under both the quota and the tariff, total consumption must also be lower under the quota. Thus, price is higher (i.e., consumer surplus is lower). Domestic profits are again higher, because they equal the same level attained under the other domestic strategy. QED

When the domestic firm chooses $x^M(k)$, the market price is higher and the domestic output level is lower under the market-share quota than under an equally restrictive tariff. While the higher price for the domestic good is merely a welfare transfer from domestic consumers to the domestic producer, the home country does suffer a welfare loss due to the higher price for the foreign good. Furthermore, the reduction in domestic output under the quota creates another source of welfare loss because the domestic good bears a price in excess of its marginal cost. The home country's welfare must therefore be lower under the quota.

When the domestic firm chooses $x^N(X^E(k))$, both market price and domestic output are higher under the market-share quota than under an

22

equally restrictive tariff. The reduction in the home country's welfare due to a higher price for imports is now counterbalanced by an efficiency gain due to increased domestic output. In this situation, a qualitative welfare comparison between the quota and the tariff requires more specific cost and demand information. Based on the above discussion, we conclude:

Proposition 4: Consider a market-share quota, $k \leq k_f$. Relative to a cum-tariff (or free-trade) equilibrium where the foreign market share equals k, the home country's welfare is lower under the quota when the domestic firm chooses $x^M(k)$. Home welfare may be higher, equal, or lower under the quota when the domestic firm chooses $x^N(X^E(k))$.

Finally, consider a quota that lies <u>above</u> the free-trade foreign market share, i.e., $k > k_f$. When the quota is set at a sufficiently large market share, the domestic firm foresakes using the quota to constrain foreign sales. The domestic firm instead reverts to an "unconstrained" strategy, and a unique pure-strategy equilibrium occurs at the free-trade equilibrium, $(x_f, X_f) = (x^N(X_f), X^N(x_f))$. Of course, the quota is not binding in this equilibrium.

While the above situation arises when the quota is <u>substantially</u> above the free-trade market share, a far different outcome occurs when the quota is reduced to a level that is closer to the free-trade market share. In fact, <u>there exists a range of quota levels above the free-trade foreign market share where no pure-strategy equilibrium occurs. Only a mixed-strategy equilibrium occurs in which the quota is binding with positive probability.</u> Thus, an "apparently nonbinding" quota may alter strategic behavior in a manner that makes the quota binding.

Proposition 5: There exists $\epsilon > 0$, such that a pure-strategy equilibrium is precluded for a market-share quota k, where $k_f < k < k_f + \epsilon$. A unique mixed-strategy equilibrium exists with properties identical to those described in Proposition 2. In this equilibrium, the quota is binding whenever the domestic firm sets output at $x^M(k)$.

Proof: Consider a quota set at the free-trade market share, k_f. Under this quota, if the foreign firm chooses its free-trade output X_f, then the optimal domestic reply is $x^M(k_f)$, where $x^M(k_f) < x^N(X_f)$.[24] Hence, $\pi^Q(x^M(k_f), X_f, k_f) > \pi^Q(x^N(X_f), X_f, k_f)$. Since $\pi^Q(x, X, k)$ is continuous in all arguments, and since $x^M(k)$ is continuous, there exists $\epsilon > 0$ such that $\pi^Q(x^M(k), X_f, k) > \pi^Q(x^N(X_f), X_f, k)$ for $k_f < k < k_f + \epsilon$. Since $x^N(X_f)$ is not an optimal reply to X_f for $k_f < k < k_f + \epsilon$, the free-trade output combination, $(x_f, X_f) = (x^N(X_f), X^N(x_f))$, is not a possible pure-strategy equilibrium when k lies within this range. All other possibilities for a pure-strategy equilibrium are eliminated by the proof to Proposition 1; however, the proof to Proposition 2 establishes a mixed-strategy equilibrium.[25] QED

5. Multimarket Sales by the Foreign Firm with Fungible Output

This section considers whether the above results are significantly altered if the foreign firm serves another market in addition to the home country's market. To distinguish this model from the prior version, we

---

[24] The free-trade equilibrium satisfies $(x_f, X_f) = (x^N(X_f), X^N(x_f))$. Given that the foreign market share equals k_f in this equilibrium, it follows that $x_f = x^N(X_f) = x^Q(X_f, k_f)$. Since $\pi^Q(x, X_f, k_f)$ is convex in the neighborhood of $x^Q(X_f, k_f)$, we conclude that $x^N(X_f)$ (i.e., $x^Q(X_f, k_f)$) is not an optimal reply to X_f. Hence, by Lemma 2, the optimal reply must be $x^M(k_f)$.

[25] Since $x^M(k)$ is the unique optimal reply to X_f, we conclude from Lemma 2 that $X^E(k) < X_f$. Given this result, the proof to Proposition 2 est` lishes the existence of a mixed-strategy equilibrium.

assume that output can be transferred (costlessly) across markets.

Under these conditions, a mixed-strategy equilibrium may still arise that is qualitatively similar to that obtained in the previous section. Alternatively, a pure-strategy equilibrium may arise where the domestic firm sets output at $x^M(k)$, and foreign sales to the home country are constrained by the quota at $X^Q(x^M(k),k)$. All remaining foreign output is sold to other markets. In this case, the imposition of a market-share quota leads to an outcome where the domestic and foreign firms split monopoly profits according to the market shares given by the quota. Compared to an equally restrictive tariff, welfare is unambiguously lower in the home country under the quota. Domestic and foreign output are relatively lower under the quota, which imply that prices are relatively higher in the home market. Although consumers are hurt by the higher prices, the domestic firm still receives higher profits under the quota.

If the foreign firm sells output to other markets, and if that output can potentially be redirected to the home market, then that output may be used as "inventories" to discourage "opportunistic" behavior by the domestic firm in the home market. For instance, when the domestic firm reduces its output to $x^M(k)$ in response to the quota, the foreign firm desires to reduce its allocation for the home market to the quota limit, $X^Q(x^M(k),k)$. In our previous model where output could not be transferred across markets, the foreign firm could achieve this outcome only by reducing its output for the home market to $X^Q(x^M(k),k)$. If the foreign firm did act in this manner, however, the domestic firm would recognize that foreign sales to the home market were effectively constrained at this output level. In response, the domestic firm would act "opportunistically" by boosting output and abandoning quota protection. Due to this probable reaction by the domestic firm, the foreign firm could not reduce its allocation for the home market to $X^Q(x^M(k),k)$. Consequently, the possibility of a pure-strategy equilibrium was eliminated in our previous model.

In contrast, when output can be transferred across markets, the foreign firm can potentially react to any domestic output expansion by transferring output into the home market. If the foreign firm can credibly transfer substantial output into the home market, then the domestic firm will keep its output at $x^M(k)$ and split monopoly profits even when it observes that the foreign firm has allocated $X^Q(x^M(k),k)$ to the home market. In this case, a pure-strategy equilibrium occurs. Otherwise, a mixed-strategy equilibrium occurs similar to that described previously.

Thus, the equilibrium outcome depends on how much output can be credibly transferred between markets by the foreign firm. This is determined by the behavior of the foreign firm's marginal revenue function in its various markets, which, in turn, depends on demand conditions and the degree of competition in those markets. If the foreign firm's marginal revenue function is relatively flat in markets outside of the home country (possibly due to increased competition), then any expansion in domestic output above $x^M(k)$ would potentially lead to a considerable expansion in the foreign firm's sales to the home market. This behavior makes it less profitable for the domestic firm to deviate from $x^M(k)$, and leads to a pure-strategy equilibrium.[26] If, however, the foreign firm's marginal revenue function is relatively steep in its overseas markets, then the foreign firm

---

[26] In fact, a pure-strategy equilibrium is necessarily obtained when the foreign firm is a price taker in its other markets.

loses substantial revenue in those markets by transferring a significant amount of output into the home country. Since the foreign firm would not transfer much output under these circumstances, the domestic firm would earn higher profits by deviating from $x^M(k)$ after observing the foreign reaction to that output choice. A pure-strategy equilibrium is not attainable in this case; instead, a mixed-strategy equilibrium exists (that is similar to the equilibrium described in the previous section).

To demonstrate the above result, let the foreign firm serve one market in addition to the home country's market. The domestic firm and the foreign firm choose output simultaneously in the first stage, but the foreign firm does not divide its output between its two markets until the second stage.[27] Since the foreign firm allocates its output to each market after the domestic firm makes its output decision, the foreign firm acts essentially as a Stackelberg follower in the second stage. In turn, the domestic firm uses its output choice in a fashion similar to a Stackelberg leader, realizing that changes in its output may subsequently alter the foreign firm's allocation between markets.[28]

Assuming that marginal costs are constant,[29] let Z_l denote the quantity of foreign sales at which marginal revenue equals marginal cost in

[27] If the foreign firm must make a binding output allocation to each market at the same time that the domestic firm chooses its output, then the outcome is identical to our previous results.

[28] Note that the Stackelberg aspects of the present model share certain similarities with the pure Stackelberg model of Mai and Hwang (1989). Under appropriate conditions, it will be shown that similar results are achieved. However, the simultaneous output decisions in the first stage of the present model are analogous to the structure of our prior model. Under appropriate conditions, it will be shown that the present model also produces analogous results to that model.

[29] This assumption does not qualitatively affect the results.

the foreign firm's other market.[30]   Under the market-share quota, the foreign output reaction function in the first stage, $X^{R\prime}(x,k)$, is described as follows:

$$X^{R\prime}(x,k) = X^R(x,k) + Z_I,$$

$$\text{where } X^R(x,k) = X^Q(x,k) \qquad\qquad \text{for } x < x^*(k)$$

$$= X^N(x) \qquad\qquad \text{for } x \geq x^*(k). \qquad (12)$$

Except for the addition of the constant Z_I, this reaction function is identical to the foreign reaction function, $X^R(x,k)$, described in Lemma 1.

The above result can be explained as follows.   The foreign firm attempts to equate marginal revenue with marginal cost in each market, except that the quota may prevent this outcome in the home market.   When the quota is not an effective constraint, the foreign sells $X^N(x)$ to the home market and Z_I to the other market.   Total output therefore equals $X^N(x) + Z_I$.   When the quota is an effective constraint, the foreign firm cannot equate marginal revenue with marginal cost in the home market.   The foreign firm sells $X^Q(x,k)$ to the home market and Z_I to the other market; hence, total output equals $X^Q(x,k) + Z_I$.

Turning to the domestic reaction function, the domestic firm realizes that an increase in its output will cause the foreign firm to allocate a larger share of its output to the home market whenever the quota constraint is "binding" (i.e., whenever the foreign firm's marginal revenue in the home market at the quota limit exceeds its marginal revenue in its other market in selling the balance of its output).   In contrast, an increase in the

---

[30]   If rival firms exist in the other market, then their output is held constant for purposes of this analysis.

domestic firm's output will cause the foreign firm to allocate a smaller share of its output to the home market whenever the quota constraint is "nonbinding" (i.e., whenever the foreign firm is able to equate marginal revenue across markets).[31] Thus, similarly to our prior model, there exists a threshold level of domestic output where the domestic firm changes its conjecture concerning the response of foreign sales to an increase in its output. The domestic firm's conjecture is positive at output levels below this threshold, but the domestic firm's conjecture is negative at output levels above this threshold. Again, the domestic firm's conjecture declines once the threshold level is attained.

This negative change in the domestic firm's conjecture implies that the domestic profit function is again convex at the threshold level of domestic output. Two possible strategies, a best "constrained" strategy and a best "unconstrained" strategy, may potentially maximize domestic profits. The domestic firm's best "constrained" output choice is $x^M(k)$, and its best "unconstrained" choice is $x^{N'}(X')$ (which solves the domestic firm's first-order condition in the absence of a quota constraint), where X' is total foreign output.

We denote the first-stage Cournot equilibrium under free trade as (x_f, X'_f); it necessarily holds that $x_f = x^{N'}(X'_f)$ in this equilibrium. When a market-share quota is imposed at or below the free-trade foreign market share, $x^{N'}(X'_f)$ is no longer an optimal domestic reply to X'_f. Instead, the optimal domestic reply is the best constrained output choice $x^M(k)$, where

---

[31] When the quota is nonbinding, the foreign firm maximizes profits by equating its marginal revenue across markets. If the domestic firm expands its output, then the foreign firm's marginal revenue declines in the home market. To re-equate marginal revenue, the foreign firm would react by transferring output away from the home market.